POLAROIDS

Superimposure one or more shots in which one photographic image is printed on top of another, as in ghost effects, titles, etc.
subjective camera

POLAROIDS

Lillian Nećakov

Coach House Books

Second printing, August 1998

CANADIAN CATALOGUING IN PUBLICATION DATA

Nećakov, Lillian, 1960-
Polaroids

2nd ed.
Poems.
ISBN 1-55245-006-6

I. Title.

PS8577.E33P64 1997 C811'.54 C97-930467-9
PR9199.3.N42P64 1997

Printed in Canada

"There is no action where there is no danger"
Howard Hawks

need for shooting the sequences involved a
striking sound which is used to emphasise
stock shot: footage of locales, action, or the like,
drawn from film libraries to eliminate the

Riding the Train with Bruno Ganz

You were never as vicious
riding the train with cobalt petals streaming from your temple
a regular fatalist swooning up against me
with your brackish breath stirring me up
bowling me over with your divinely lit eyes
up and down the corroded tracks of their dated city
gentle in your foreignness coping
disembarrassed extinct and exact in your authentic mode
smiling down from the stars
a dusty angel crushing down on my rib cage
popularizing the love of fear
through a thousand stages

you were never my hero for even a second
until you climbed back into my permanent dreaming
unshaven and nostalgic tasting of naphthalene
combing my hair with heavy germanic strokes
travelling one station at a time into some sort of morbid
onslaught of women in rippled blouses laughing
at the luxurious daffodils you arranged at my feet
once there you steam-rollered my heart and sucked
at the crimson fittings around it
gushing with piety you stormed into my private season
and cursed me with the kind of love that fuses to the bone
once.

Polaroids of Tobe Hooper

Once all the bruises were worn through
and you slid into the beach chair
the wind changed direction
calmed your matted hair
into one solid clump of disaster
skin-fulls of the nastiness oozing from your
smile
guru-fish, spider monkey, loser
all glowing full of widow's grief and passion
masked with frenzy
posing the pose
a camera never spies incorrectly
salt lick lens under your nostrils
you are a beautiful pigeon
mocking our tastelessly attired bones.

Harry Dean Stanton at the El Rancho Motel

After Wim Wenders' Paris, Texas 1984

Remember when you, way down inside
changed your mind about the way you read the lightning
remember how you told me change was life in the pocket
and if I stayed still too long
eventually the thunder would strike all my rivers
and I would be left behind on a raft of dried poppies

remember why you pointed your barograph
to the eastern skies
predicting my downfall
on a mechanical night in February
when you swore I would lose momentum and derail
and they would find me frozen under a gravel pillow

remember when you found me wandering the desert
in shoes that had outgrown me
with curious voices pasted against my head
running towards the thick sun
remember how you found me through a thousand grains of sand
occupied with my own speechlessness
crimson hat bobbing against a windless sky
moving
moving because remember you told me
moving was remembrance moving itself moving
was because you told me remember
moving?

Lili Taylor Stands Under a Lamppost in Small-Town America

After Nancy Savoca's Dogfight 1991

Lili Taylor stands under a lamppost in small-town America
waves at the bus full of army boys with pale fingers
touches the back of her leg
counts her dog bites
on cool summer evenings like this she is it
what they've been dreaming of while polishing boots

Lili Taylor lifts her crinoline over her head
the bet is on
her dog bites are perfect
her face finds his
he pulls her close to him and begins the lie

Lili Taylor dances with her army boy
up close
she knows she is not it
he is dancing to a slightly different rhythm
for a slightly different girl waiting
at the edge of the war

Lili Taylor wins all bets
he falls to his knees years later
dreams of her often
runs his pale fingers up the back of his arm
feels for the teeth marks
counts.

Angels

After Wim Wenders' Wings of Desire 1988

He is an American angel
on the other side of the ocean
on the other side of the wall
come to steal their wings

he flutters past abandoned fields
wet with rain
begins a fairy tale of life
where he is no longer an angel
where he stands above the city looking down
with eyes that have never closed without sleep

he is an American angel
come to steal their thunder
while they stroke each other's wings at the ending of the day
he is an American wandering their set
swaggering past the ruins of their dreams
he is Peter Falk dressed as Colombo
impersonating an angel
impersonating an American full of desire
to fly over their heavens with foreign wings.

Moth Catcher

After Billy Wilder's Sunset Blvd. 1950

What happens when they find me floating past the lilies
face down in her pool?
well that's where it begins
the story of me and Norma
somewhere between her stairway and the street
from the moment she stepped out of the light
and spiraled her way toward me
in a river of perfumed desire
a serpent of gargantuan proportions cluttering my vision
inviting me to lie at the bottom of the stairs
to watch her dance the dance of forgotten women

what happens when you fall for it?
when you find yourself in her arms
with the credits rolling
and you realize there is no moth catcher with his flood lights
waiting to catch your fall
there is no you and Norma at the bottom of the stairs
there is only a faint trace of a swan opening its wings

what happens is they find you on a bed of seaweed swooning
against her scent.

The Journey

After Jane Campion's <u>The Piano</u> 1993

Midnight and long ships have brought her to him
journeying over the rivers of time
she arrives on deserted beaches until

what he hears are her fingers stroking the keys
then ribbons of unimaginable happiness
slip through his hands
falling at her feet music crashes into him
from every direction

midnight and the forest takes her away from him until
she arrives again days later
to lie with him under the heavy palms under his piano until
he understands the journey of her silence until
he speaks from a place of unimaginable rapture until
the long ships take them to the very bottom of the ocean
where the echo of his voice will fade from her lips.

Hal Hartley on a Harley

I could have sworn I saw Hal Hartley on a Harley
going up and down Church St.
I could have sworn I saw Hal Hartley on a Harley
going up and down Church St.

I could have sworn he said he found the truth
the unbelievable truth in 11 days
on Long Island with a film crew shooting day and night
and the rain coming down in buckets
that he actually knew what it was all about
life, I mean
on a Harley
on Church St. Hal smiles
offers up some advice
says "don't even climb a tree at night"
and we all laugh like
we really know what he means
when we don't know what the hell he's talking about
but hey he's Hal Hartley
but hey he's Hal Hartley
and he sure knows how to point that camera our way.

Three Losers in Louisiana

After Jim Jarmusch's Down By Law 1986

He can't even fry up an egg but he sure knows murder
rumour has it he killed a guy with an eight ball
threw it right at his head
and now he's locked up with two losers
with only a deck of cards between them
and big dreams of Walt Whitman

escape costs nothing
once their feet touch the earth it's simple
they move north out of the bayou
he recites Bob Frost and tells the losers
that America is for poets
and that his name is Roberto but they can call him Bob
he delivers them to a clearing where the road forks
"the world is a strange and beautiful place"he tells them
"wish you were here"

the losers turn their backs on him
move towards the dull sun and whisper "buzz off".

The Whole Damn Story

After Fred Coe's A Thousand Clowns 1965

Nick goes by Dr. Morris Fishburne, Chevrolet
and Rudolfo
Nick is 12, lives with Murray on the east side
and has to choose between truth and faith
and finally a name to go by

Nick and Murray wander through abandoned chinese restaurants
collecting photographs of faded dynasties
and discarded bus tickets
on warm spring nights Murray tells Nick the story

the story of Nick and Murray and the whole damn thing
and what Nick just can't understand is why she left
why, if she roams the very same earth he does
can't he find her footsteps and follow them
to where he would find her and read to her
from day-old newspapers until they would fall to the ground
in hysterics

Nick sleeps on the fire-escape with a picture
of her face
and wakes to the sound of Murray stretching canvas
painting the entire story of Nick and Murray and the whole damn thing

Nick is 12 and crawls through Murray's imagination
looking for clues of their past and present
and shops around for language that will fill Murray with happiness
finds a single word
"absent".

Hammett in Hollywood

After W. S. Van Dyke's The Thin Man 1934

Asta keeps Nora hopping
between martinis

after walking the pooch Nora reclines
in her satin dressing gown with that face
that keeps us all at the edge of our seats
waiting for the thin man to step out of his shadow
and tell us how we figure into it

between martinis he steps into the picture
unravels the mystery of America right up there on the screen
just as if it all came down to Hammett typing
what we were all feeling at that very instant.

Tango

After Alfred Hitchcock's Rope 1948

The body can't come between them
what's done is done
and soon the whole gang will come through the door
fedoras afloat
pass the cheese and I know who done it

murder is a six letter word for fun
that's all
his heart has stopped because of them
because boys know how to use rope
to make their dreams come true
to make their eyes wild above his gasps
boys know what other boys feel
like a syringe climbing up the vein

the guests arrive in colour
the body knows its place
no one is invited to tango.

Werner Has Gone Mad

After Les Blank's <u>Burden of Dreams</u> 1982

Les writes letters from the Amazon
he's waiting for coffee
Werner has gone mad
he's dragging ships across mountains
they compare tattoos

Werner writes letters to his parents
the jungle is in him
the heat like arrows in the flesh
is necessary

Les photographs the burden of Werner's dreams
while no letters arrive home
Werner tells us the devil is right here
speaking to us in jungle language

Werner photographs collective murder
crazed by the wrath of his imaginings he drops us
into a steamboat of catastrophe
spinning wildly downstream
and lets us into our own seasons of hell

Les and Werner have made the trip
they have documented the trance
the jungle is woven up inside them
they will carry it with them like an opera
on the very tip of their hearts.

The French Love Buddy Love

After Jerry Lewis's The Nutty Professor 1963

Every Frenchman holds Buddy in his heart
next to Apollinaire and Tzara
because they know that Buddy started it all
the real surrealist revolution in France
between sets down at the night club
between playing teacher and running with the rat pack
Buddy is the cause of all their anxiety
the reason they all speak in such tiny whispers
and mime their way out of their collective guilt

the French love Buddy Love
because he comes to them in technicolour
his face beaming on the covers of trashy magazines
Buddy occupies a place in their conscience
where hollywood is king
they love Buddy despite themselves
while Paris burns they scramble to collect their ticket stubs
to catch the last re-run of Buddy's transformation
from surrealist heart throb to professor of angst

Buddy loves the French because they pay his bills
he doesn't give a damn who owns history
or hollywood or the cameras
he combs his hair straight up
three times a day
doesn't speak a word of foreign
and eats chinese take-out
Buddy is America's worst nightmare.

A Procession of Travelers

After Terrence Malick's Days of Heaven 1978

During the days and nights of heaven
we ride the river looking for the light
in each other's eyes
arms extended we reach for reflections on the water
and find the faces of strangers that have crossed the stars before us

on land we travel slower
finding fewer reminders of ourselves
settling the west with dreams of locusts
and indigo sky

flames of wheat pierce our hearts
and open us up to the spirits
while we gather the dust and rain
a procession of travelers mimic the storm
skirts billow under the planets

a kind of copper moon falls our way.

Hoagy Carmichael Steals the Show

After Howard Hawks' To Have and Have Not 1944

Harry's fingers move into the shot
the credits roll
Bacall steps in with that voice
and we're on our way
watching them fall for each other right up there
in 1944 in black and white and Hoagy pounding the piano
it's like going down the road a hundred miles an hour
with the moon all lit up and the stars bending down on you
cooling the night
it's like the time you were nine and dreamed of dancing
on the edge of the earth with a bag full of crickets
it's like all the times you wanted to feel happy and actually did
like skating on a lake full of frozen faces looking up at you
a kind of calm filling you up inside
it's like day and night and all the in between
only this time Hoagy Carmichael steals the show.

Another Cowboy in Hamburg

After Wim Wenders' The American Friend 1977

Dennis Hopper walks into your shop
and wants to be your American friend
just like that
he takes you through your own streets
trying to convince you he's not just another cowboy
in a language you recall from your childhood
a language that occupied you for days
long after the gangsters had moved off the screen

Dennis Hopper steals your heart
on a night-train moving out of Hamburg
with murder on his breath
he dishes out plenty of suspense
slicks back his hair and repeats it all once more
just in case you weren't looking
it's his way of working the room

you want to be Dennis's friend
only it doesn't make sense
he's all pulp fiction
a hero in the making
imitating the way your lips move
trying on your past just for size

Dennis Hopper walks into your life
finds you driving around in circles
on a deserted beach
your hands covered in gold leaf
you ask him why
he wants to be your friend
he looks out at the ocean and says
"isn't that enough?"

Cab Ride

After Jim Jarmusch's Night on Earth 1991

There are nights on earth when a cab ride is all it takes
to reveal the entire truth
about where we are going and at what speed

there are five stories for each lie we tell
and there are never enough names for us to slide into
not enough cities or streets to hide in
while the meter runs on and on
we journey past the horror of our loneliness
and into someone else's continent
someone else's version of the very same story
we've been telling each other for years

our lives move in sequence from one shot to the next
subtitled and more offensive than we would have liked
our blood is full of burden
the burden of drowning sheep.

Perhan's Dream

After Emir Kusturica's Time of the Gypsies 1989

When the rooster crows
they will place a gold coin on each of his dead eyes
the sun will set before the dance is done
on the seventh day they will mourn him
with trumpets and flirting for the last time

Perhan's dream never ends
night after night the moon slips into his bed
filling his head with unimaginable stories of chaos
it is only when he wakes that Perhan stands on his own two feet
and looks at himself flying across the highways
humming a tiny gypsy song.

Sleeping with the Preacher

After Charles Laughton's The Night of the Hunter 1955

Preacher Harry Powell does god's work
down in the barn's where they found the last one
the sixth, maybe the twelfth, preacher can't recall
all's he knows is how to talk to god
and that there ain't but one word for what these women want
evil comes to him down by the river
he hunts down the night
and tattoos his fingers for the lord

love and hate come from the same exact place
flesh and blood
and there is no word for a child's fear
there is a body at the bottom of the river
blessed by the preacher
lying with the angels
singing hymns
hounded day and night by the hunter
sleeping with the preacher.

Confession

After Martin Scorsese's Raging Bull 1980

From the fifth row you can see blood coming off the rope
silence
then the flashbulbs
a glove-full of punishment
a left hook
fifteen rounds of rage
and the camera always stays in the ring with Jake

there are forces of evil that move him
into spheres of such great anger
that a bloody sponge is his only confession

Jake crushes the world
fights like he deserves to die
and beats on his wife
because she is exactly what he wants to be

for Jake there is no real enemy
no rehearsal
just his own heart stopping for a moment
as the lights come up
and he fall to his knees
silver trunks
and the eyes of an angel.

The Postman

After Jean-Jacques Beineix's Diva 1982

The Marx brothers storm the opera house
Jules is stealing the diva's voice
delivering her love letters from the street

homicide is carried out on mopeds
while the postman rewinds his tape
to a precise moment in time
where he can picture himself with her
under an umbrella tearing open letters from strangers
writing to tell him that they too carry her voice
in a satchel through the crowds

the postman walks with lovely girls but dreams of his diva
all dark and elaborate with ruthless thievery on her mind
stealing the vessel in which his heart once swam
she hits the highest note
collapses at his feet in her zen-coloured gown.

Long Distance

After Francis Coppola's Apocalypse Now 1979

I can't believe I called you up in the middle of the night
long distance
to read you a poem
when I should have been telling you
about my journey to the midnight of the soul
in the front row of the movie theatre with my head craned back
and how after that there was nowhere else left to go
I should have been asking you about who really won the war
you would have steered me straight and maybe even out
of my darkest heart
into a place where the river would stop
and spread its corpse out to dry

weeks later I crawl out of bed and think of the metal horses of war
and how we all create our own hell
then join up and kill whatever's left
whatever resembles ourselves
I pinpoint the source of my guilt
and it's not really that I called you up in the middle of some night
with poetry on my mind
it's that I know what it means to hate
and that I understand the horrific journey of our lives
and how it ends with mockery
and a heart full of the beast.

Huckleberry

After George P. Cosmatos' Tombstone 1993

Doc pours himself another round
feels the cool metal against his rib cage
fingers the trigger and the jig is up
Earp can't shoot even near as straight as he can piss
and Doc's his only hope
but Doc's got cards and whiskey so deep in his veins
that getting up out of those TB sheets some mornings
makes him wish Arizona was just a dream
but it's not that simple
Doc writes books on death and friendship
and tells Earp that some men need revenge
just for being born

dust fills his lungs
he loads his 12 gauge
and travels to a place where he can prove friendship
just with the tip of a hat
and a bullet
Doc fancies the dawn
and wakes to his own voice whispering
"I'm here huckleberry".

Through the Cathedral

After Michael Cimino's Heaven's Gate 1980

The gates of heaven open
onto a hundred crows lying in golden dust
smiling at our misfortunes

Wyoming combs its smoke-filled days
through our hair
the whistle sparks the giant heart of hope
our train pulls into a dream of the west
we once had while cradled in our mothers' sorrows

the tongue is a tool that shapes all the imaginings
of our childhood into a single word that catches
in the heart of every stranger that gives us the pistol

what a man can never trust is the land
or his secret heart
and what's left at the end of the day is this
a sky full of sheets blowing back and forth
reminding him of heaven and the saints
and a language he once carried
through a cathedral
full of men and women wearing his very skin.

Fan Mail

After Bertrand Blier's Too Beautiful For You 1989

Before you were born I used to get fan mail
in one letter it said that I had been spotted
at the cinema
I was seen sitting in the middle of the third row
on the coldest night of the year
he thought I may have been taking notes
analyzing the performance or writing love letters
while Depardieu pulled his pants down
to convince her that there was hope in longing
and that he carried her song in his chest
that the night belonged to her if she wanted it
and that a Frenchman knows the rooms where women wander
collecting words which are too beautiful to be spoken

he thought I may have hung my head in sorrow
or nostalgia or that my heart may have been touched
by the desire of a large man
lost on a joyless highway looking for enchantment

it never occurred to me that anyone may have thought
I would have been taken by it all
I just needed a dark place to sit
and clip the wings of a butterfly
while a distant light flickered all around me
just enough to remind me of you.

Hawks Directs

After Howard Hawks' Rio Bravo 1959

Feathers saves the day
she rides into town all dressed as Angie Dickinson
taking the sheriff for a spin
while Hawks directs the last stand off
it's not that Ricky Nelson can really sing
it's that Dean plays a mean drunk
and I just can't get him off my mind

Walter Brennan's toothless banter sends me
I know it's pure Furthman and the language flies
I'm in love with the sunsets and dust and Wayne
playing himself one more time
and I know that if I could have anything
it would be to have been born just a year or two before
my birthday
so that I could dip my fingers in the trough
after a long day on the set and head directly to the saloon
for a P.O.V. shot of myself
lost in the best damn western around.

Cancelling Out the Bad Guys

After Mark L. Lester's Commando 1985

He asks me who the hell writes this stuff
like it's not funny
he just doesn't get it
Arnold's all in a tizzy, someone's got his daughter
and he has to fight off the entire U.S. just to get her back
but I tell him it's not the action
listen to the lines they never stop cutting you up
like we need another action hero he tells me
but that's not the point
Arnie's got the comic books beat, he's our last hope
we need a new funny man to lead us into a fantasy
of ourselves pulling up in terrific sports car
jumping off of cliffs to catchy tunes
while the entire world spins out of orbit
and into the next most boring century we've ever seen
it's all poetic justice with Arnie cancelling out the bad guys
and making us feel all warm and fuzzy
in front of everyone
and it can't get more embarrassing than that.

Slow-Motion

After Jean Vigo's Zero de Conduite 1933

Here's the thing
I was going through some movie stills
and I found one, of the final shot
of a film I saw at least a decade before I ever met you

four boys climbing the roof of the school house
a victorious gang of rebels soaring up to the heavens
with nothing on their minds
arms raised like Esther Williams about to dive into a pool
of diamonds and feathers

years before I had known your voice, I heard it
in slow-motion
during the same film on a friday morning
with the snow coming in on northern wings
spilling its contents down on us
thousands of tiny frozen finger nails
on our landscape
reminding us of the most important scene
when the boys rip open a room full of pillows
and find a kind of silent grace in their flowering.

The Concubine

After Zhang Yimou's Raise the Red Lantern 1991

When her lantern is lit
he will come to her at dusk with the hands of a ploughman
wrapped in white ribbons
and smelling of a previous love
he will call her once by a name she has never before heard
and it will echo through her memory looking for a place to rest
finally she will lie next to his heaving shoulders
and wipe away his oceans of fear
she will collect the salt from his weeping heart
in one hand
before the light reaches her door

he will separate his shadow from hers
and place an orchid across her slippers
leaving her forever until the next time
she will search for him during white nights
on endless rooftops
and she will always be the last river he comes to
after all the lanterns of his soul have been scattered
against a frigid horizon.

The Two Edies

After David and Albert Maysles' Grey Gardens 1976

Little Edie and big Edie roam their 28 rooms
in East Hampton until their secret is discovered
one hot September day
on the terrace of a rotting mansion filled with jingoism

the camera never moves, it is Little Edie who dances
in and out of frame
head always covered
a saintly dove gone haywire
wings flapping out of control
imagining herself someday as Big Edie
wading in a pool of tin cans
casting a giant shadow on the walls of her fortress

the public love the Edies
and what's not to like
a mother and daughter who fire up their fog machine
and rile up the entire nation with a little two-step
while feeding raccoons in the attic of a house
whose spirits line the steps waiting for their fall.

The Fury

After Ridley Scott's The Duellists 1977

They have come across the moors of time
to court each other's fury
with long sabers made of moonbeams
they will duel through the eternities of rain
until the wars of Napoleon come calling
and their magic ends on a hill-top
with the logic of images
set to a hauntingly silent score.

Just a Bit Cold Around the Heart

After Joel Coen's Blood Simple 1984

It must have been about twelve years ago or so
I don't really remember
all I know is that Eli say's "kid, you gotta see this film
it'll tear your guts out"

turns out it's a modern day noir classic
with a knife in the heart
and the lighting comes close to Hitchcock
it's all about love and betrayal and murder
and digging your own grave in the middle of the night
in a deserted field feeling the rhythm of your killer's pulse
it's like taking a dip in a pool of sweat that's gone and frozen
and you come out of it all thinking
that you're just a bit cold around the heart.

Forgotten Bride

After Robert Flaherty's Man of Aran 1934

Flaherty's camera caresses rock and ocean
sky and fisherman
small boats weave in and out of the mountainous waves
the nets are laid out to dry under an unfaithful sun
like a forgotten bride

the storms stir the spirit to hunt
harpoons spear the salty colossus and find a home
in the belly of a shark
while women look for cardigans
among the tide's remains

there is great clarity in his vision
and the roar of the soul is never aloud even a peep
we are left standing on cliffs of such passion
that it is only years later that we discover
he has won our souls out of us.

Yikes! It's All a Bit Too Kitsch

After Michael Gordon's Pillow Talk 1959

Yikes! it's all a bit too kitsch
Doris and Rock hanging out talking on the phone in CinemaScope
with Tony Randall playing interference
it's party line time and Doris hasn't a clue about Rock
I mean she just hasn't got a clue
she's all cute and bubbly lounging on a sea of pillows
waiting for the call to trigger her into action
the scene goes all soft focus and we melt
despite ourselves
despite the fact that this ain't the first time we've been jerked around
by hollywood and lead into a fairy tale we can't escape
despite Rock and his cad-like ways
despite ourselves and Doris and Tony and Rock and the plushness
of it all
we choke back another coke and climb into our fuzzy slippers
rewind the VCR for another shot at the chance to play house.

Pigs and Pearls

After Dusan Makavejev's Montenegro 1981

The monkey's in his cage
our lungs are full of middle-class
we are drowning in the dreams of primates
and down the road there is a woman slicing up roast pig
to the sounds of "Gimme a Little Kiss"
everyone dances with their own exile
it's a better life with a knife in the head
snapping photos of cruel ice-kings
Stockholm allows no one to sleep in her arms
east meets west on neutral ground
blood boils, curdles and we go back
to our saintly lives
with a little tiny pagan spot on our shoes
which we scrub but can't remove
it becomes the only constant in our search
for a paradise roaring with wind.

Cutting Bone

After Ivan Passer's Cutter's Way 1981

We are dead stars
climbing onto crosses eluding rescue
the parade passes through us without notice
the flamenco dancer lifts her heels
to the rhythm of our decay
it's another day that we leave a strip of flesh
on the bathroom door hook
with bastards like us who needs saviours.

My Whole Life

After Martin Scorsese's The King of Comedy 1983

Rup is a full-time nobody
white shoes and checkers
he's just the kind of loud punishment we need
he wants his shot at the big time
it's a two-way street
friendship
coming to you via satellite
on every channel
and if you don't want any part of it
Rup will sure tell you otherwise
see, he's the real funny guy
and his whole life's on the rejection list
step on his toes and he'll replace you so fast
you won't even have time to taste the ugliness
of his smile.

Morocco

After Josef Von Sternberg's Morocco 1930

Marlene sings three numbers
kisses the lips of many men
tips her top-hat in the direction of charming girls
and dances through Moroccan dunes
with a twisted tongue
she banishes us all
she is the next ripple in Joe's calm
and when he moves to light her
she lets him comb back a strand of hair
but always chooses her soldier over him

the desert is a cabaret of footprints
she finds his imprint and fills it
with a mischievous glance
and continues into the sunset
with her back to Joe and all of Hollywood.

Somewhere Will Rogers is Smiling

After Bob Clark's A Christmas Story 1983

All I kept hearing my entire childhood was
"you'll put your eye out"
as if there were more to life than a Red Ryder BB gun
as if it wasn't enough that parts of my soul were still frozen
to the school-yard fence in some tiny mid-west town

all I know is that one winter morning finally
an angel brushed up against me
snow drifts climbed up the side of our house
and Will Rogers held my hand steady
as I fired my Red Ryder across the street
into my entire future.

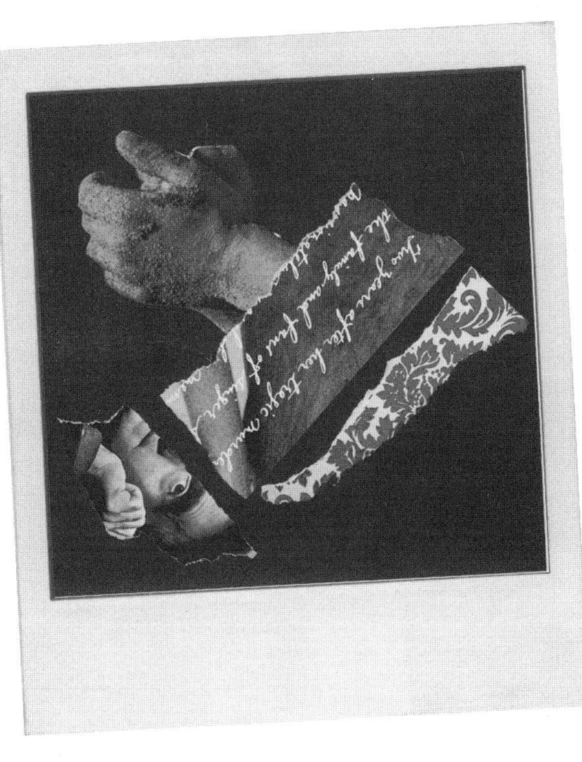

Two years after her tragic
the family and fear of

The first edition of 250 copies
was set in Meta Plus and printed on Zephyr Narrow Laid stock
at Coach House Printing on bpNichol Lane
in June of 1997.

Subplot. a story-within-a-story;
characters and developed ...
LOOK SHARPER THAN OTHERS.